But there are no new ideas waiting in the wings to save us as women, as human. There are only old and forgotten ones, new combinations, extrapolations and recognitions from within ourselves, along with the renewed courage to try them out.

—Audre Lorde
"Poems Are Not Luxuries"

Claiming
an Identity

P E R S E P H O N E   P R E S S

Watertown, Massachusetts

Michelle Cliff

They Taught Me to Despise

"Obsolete Geography" first appeared in *Conditions,* no. 3;
"Accurate Record" in the August, 1978, issue of *Sojourner;*
"A History of Costume" in *Conditions,* no. 4; "Against
Granite" in *Heresies,* issue 8; and "Claiming an Identity
They Taught Me to Despise" in *Azalea,* vol. 3, no. 1.

Cover design by Maria von Brincken.
Text design by Pat McGloin.

Library of Congress Cataloging in Publication Data

Cliff, Michelle.
    Claiming an identity they taught me to despise.

    I. Title.
PS3553.L437C55   811'.54   80-23137
ISBN 0-930436-06-7 (pbk.)

First Edition. First Printing.

in memory of my great-grandmother, Rachel

ABOUT THE AUTHOR

Michelle Cliff received her M.Phil. in comparative historical studies of the Renaissance from the Warburg Institute at the University of London. Since then, her writings have appeared throughout the feminist press. Her first book, *The Winner Names the Age: A Collection of Writings by Lillian Smith* (W.W. Norton & Co.), received wide acclaim.

Claiming an Identity They Taught Me to Despise

Passing

I

> The mystery of the world is the visible, not the
> invisible.
>
> —Oscar Wilde

Camouflage: ground lizards in the schoolyard rustle
under a pile of leaves—some are deep-green, others
shiny blue: all blend in. I fear they might be there—
even when there is no sound.

To this day camouflage terrorizes me.

The pattern of skin which makes a being invisible
against its habitat.

And—yes—this camouflage exists for its protection.
I am not what I seem to be.

I must make myself visible against my habitat. But
there exists a certain danger in peeling back. The dia-
mondback without her mottled skin loses a level of
defense.

The onlooker may be startled to recognize the visible being.
The onlooker may react with disbelief: sometimes, with recognition.

II

I am remembering: women in Jamaica asking to touch my hair.

On a map from 1740 which hangs above my desk I can see the place where my grandmother now lives. Old-womans Savannah. That is the place which holds colors for me. The other seems a shadow-life.

I am remembering: in the hard dirt in the bright sun between the house and the shed which is a kitchen my mother sat—after church—on a wooden crate. Under the box a headless chicken flapped its wings.

Quiet. Then she rose—removed the box. Plunged the carcass into boiling water to loosen the feathers.

She passed the carcass to her mother who cut and stewed Sunday dinner.

I watched this all in wonder. The two women were almost silent.

III

I thought it was only the loss of the mother—
but it was also the loss of others:
who grew up to work for us
and stood at the doorway while the tv played

and stood at the doorway while we told ghost-stories
and ironed the cloths for the tea-trays.
but this division existed even then—

Passing demands a desire to become invisible. A ghost-
life. An ignorance of connections.

IV

In America: each year the day before school after
summer vacation I sat on my bed touching my note-
books, pencils, ruler—holding the stern and sweet-
smelling brown oxfords in my lap and spreading my
skirt and blouse and underwear and socks before me.
My mother would come in and always say the same
thing: "Free paper burn now."

Such words conspire to make a past.
Such words conjure a knowledge.
Such words make assimilation impossible. They stay
with you for years. They puzzle but you sense a signifi-
cance. I need these words.

V

People call my grandmother the miracle of the loaves
and the fishes. People used to fill the yard at dinnertime
with their enamel bowls and utensils waiting to be fed.
And she managed to feed them all. Whether rice or yam
or green banana cooked in dried saltfish.

In America this food became a secret—and a link. Shop-
ping under the bridge with my mother for cho-cho and
cassava and breadfruit. And the New Home Bakery for
hard-dough bread. Finding a woman who makes para-
dise plums.

The church we belong to is having a West Indian dinner and my mother has agreed to share her food. The church hall is crowded. But the groups do not mix. One white woman carefully removes a chewed piece of green banana from her mouth and slides it to the side of her plate.

My mother sees this. She says nothing.

Passing demands quiet. And from that quiet—silence.

VI

Something used by someone else carries a history with it. A piece of cloth, a platter, a cut-glass pitcher, a recipe.

A history and a spirit. You want to know when it was used. And how. And what it wants from you.

Passing demands you keep that knowledge to yourself.

VII

In Jamaica we are as common as ticks.
We graft the Bombay onto the common mango. The Valencia onto the Seville. We mix tangerines and oranges. We create mules.

Under British rule—Zora Neale Hurston writes about this—we could have ourselves declared legally white. The rationale was that it made us better servants.

This symbolic skin was carried to the United States where passing was easy.

6

Isolate yourself. If they find out about you it's all over. Forget about your great-grandfather with the darkest skin—until you're back "home" where they joke about how he climbed a coconut tree when he was eighty. Go to college. Go to England to study. Learn about the Italian Renaissance and forget that they kept slaves. Ignore the tears of the Indians. Black Americans don't understand us either. We are—after all—British. If anyone asks you talk about sugar plantations and the Maroons—not the landscape of downtown Kingston or the children at the roadside. Be selective. Cultivate normalcy. Stress sameness. Blend in. For God's sake don't pile difference upon difference. It's not safe.

Back on the island the deep-purple skin of the ripe fruit conceals a center which holds a star-shape. Sitting in the branches one afternoon with a friend we eat ourselves into an intimacy in which we talk about our families. He is fourteen and works for my grandmother. I am twelve. He tells me his grandmother was East Indian and therefore he is not completely black. I tell him I am white—showing my sunburnt nose—explaining only white skin burns. He laughs. Then we scuffle.

It is like trying to remember a dream in which the images slip and slide. The words connect and disconnect and you wake feeling senseless.

"No strange news" my grandmother often closes her letters.

We are not exotic—or aromatic—or poignant.
We are not aberrations. We are ordinary.
All this has happened before.

Filaments

I am untangling the filaments of my history.

I

At first: The water washed me through my mother's legs and onto the sheet of her lying-in bed. Were her thighs like white ice-cliffs? Was the water streaked with red? Or did clear water wash me through mahogany columns?

The question of my identity is partly a question of color: of my right to name myself. That is what I have felt—all along.

I dream I am on a sailing ship in the South Pacific: sailing to the South Pole. In the distance are two enormous ice-cliffs—on either side of the entrance to a harbor. The ice-cliffs rise suddenly from the water—which is green-blue. The sunlight hits the ice-faces and reflects off the water, making everything green-blue. This is the background.

In the foreground is a Polynesian woman in a dugout canoe—naked except for a black loincloth. She is caught in a whirlpool at the center of the dream and is stroking

8

her way out. As she raises the paddle of the canoe I am struck by the muscles of her upper arms: they move with her strength; her sweat makes their surfaces shine.

The ice-cliffs guard Antarctica—a domain of whiteness—but alone do not ensure the purity of the domain. They depend on the whirlpool to remove all trace of color. The whirlpool necessitates a roiling surface: the domain will not be calm. The eyes of outsiders will immediately focus on the repetitive convolutions of water.

The escape of the woman of color is assured. She is here merely to accentuate my origins: to contradict the statement of the ice-cliffs. Her loincloth—the darkest part of her—is my swaddling dress: with which my identity is tightly wrapped.

II

The scalpel slices what will become the scar.
Tracing what might have been a Caesarean birth—but isn't. I hold no child inside—only an exploded appendix spewing gangrene; due to neglect, and a wrong diagnosis.

Years later I still feel the tingle of the blade—not meant to be. Still hear my half-felt voice outside, complaining: "Something's wrong. Am I really *supposed* to feel this?"

"Oh, God," the surgeon returns. "Knock her out."

I am split—only wooden pegs and wire holding insides inside.

Early morning: my father's hands—his eyes disguised by dark glasses. His voice—telling me it's not serious.

The green sheet darkens suddenly. More darkness in the already-dark enclosure. Darkness spreads across and down as the wound resists closure. The face of a tall woman—black, mistakenly called nurse—reacts to my father's screams. Her fingers effect an intricate task. Not needlework, not tapestry exactly—merely closing up, mending, making me safe.

There is a black box beside the bed. Concealing a pump. Lights flash at intervals and I see the gangrene rushing out of me through clear plastic tubing. My capacity for poison amazes me.

One tube runs through my nose, down my throat, and continues into my stomach. I have to concentrate: Hold the tongue inside the mouth—or else the sensation is like drowning.

The morphine works wonders. I fly to the ceiling and watch my body on the bed. She's very sick, I think. At the ceiling I meet a variety of apparitions. Faces that change as I approach them. The lined faces of tribal chieftains. I need to describe this vision.

No one warned me about withdrawal. No junkie I— curled up and weeping. No Billie Holiday in her jail cell. But the tears and pain are constant.

I am out of control in front of my mother. Unable to contain my pity for her. She is in a deep depression and hasn't eaten for days. Somehow this is my fault.

I am alone and look around the room. The lilacs in the water jug wrap me in their light-purple blooms. Their heavy scent the only motion. I lie there and do not sleep. At times awake; at times drifting. There are new apparitions, but the morphine is no longer the stimulus.

The window next to the bed becomes an entrance: a tunnel slopes downward into light. There is no carved gateway but I know what this is. It would be so easy to enter. I have the stuff it takes to fly.

I look away and look again at the window. The tunnel is still there. If anything, the light is brighter. I know that passage will be irrevocable. I am forced to act. I try for pain: straining against the clamps in the incision I sit upright. I grab the lilacs and press them to my face: and breathe deep while time passes. The lilacs begin to stink. I sweat and am cold. The cut hurts. The window is once again the window.

III

In the family I was called "fair"—a hard term. My sister was darker, younger. We were split: along lines of color and order of birth.

That family surface: treacherous—always the threat the heritage would out: that blackness would rise like slick oil and coat the white feathers of seabirds. Lies were devised. Truth was reserved for dreams. Jane Eyre separated from Bertha. Vyry from Miss Lillian.

This kind of splitting breeds insanity.

IV

My father took me to see *Snow White* when I was five: I embarrassed him by crying—not believing as she lay in her glass coffin that the poisoned apple would be dislodged by the prince's kiss. We returned home, where my mother was sick with flu. *I have never seen my*

11

mother naked. I tiptoe to their bedroom door and watch her body on the pale bedspread. As I stand there his hand comes down around my neck. He chooses the punishment.

A space is left where knowledge of her body should be. I fill this space with a false knowing: I mis/take my flesh and contours for hers—my voice speaks for those parts of her she cannot reach or show. It does not end there: I become her simulacrum—an accessible representative. Until the tissue is ripped through I will swallow myself.

V

I sometimes dream of my own dismemberment: of arms and legs removed to make escape impossible. Escape: or rather separation—an earned departure.

I want to raise the handmade paddle of the dugout canoe: to have the green-blue vision tint the skin of my upper arms. To sweat freely as I remove myself under my own power. Away from the domain of the ice-cliffs—frozen into silence.

Obsolete Geography

I

Airplane shadows moved across the mountains; leaving me to clear rivers, dancing birds, sweet fruits. Sitting on a river rock, my legs dangle in the water. I am twelve—and solitary.

II

On a hillside I search for mangoes. As I shake the tree the fruit drops: its sweetness splits at my feet. I suck the remaining flesh from the hairy seed. The sap from the stem stains my lips: to fester later. I am warned I may be scarred.

III

My other life of notebooks, lessons, homework continues. I try not to pay it mind.

IV

Things that live here: star apple, pineapple, custard apple, south sea apple; tamarind, ginep, avocado, guava,

13

cashew, cane; yellow, white, St. Vincent yam; red, black, pepper ants; bats, scorpions, nightingales, spiders; cassava, sweetsop, soursop, cho-cho, okra, guango, mahoe, mahogany, ackee, plaintain, chinese banana; poly lizard, green lizard, croaking lizard, ground lizard.

V

The pig is big, and hangs suspended by her hind legs from a tree in the yard. She is screaming—her agony not self-conscious. I have been told not to watch her slaughter, but my twelve-year-old self longs for the flow of blood. A small knife is inserted in her throat, pulled back and forth; until the throat slits, the wound widens, and blood runs over, covering the yard.

As her cries cease, mine begin. I have seen other slaughters but this one will stay with me.

VI

My grandmother's verandah before they renovated the house sloped downhill. The direction the marbles took as they rolled toward the set-up dominoes was always the same. There was a particular lizard at one end, who crawled up to take the sun in the afternoon. I provoked him—knowing he had a temper, since half his tail was missing. As he got angry he turned black with rage and blew a balloon of flesh from his throat—and sat there.

VII

Sitting in the maid's room asking her about her daughter, who is somewhere else. I examine the contents of her dressing table: perfume, comb, hand-mirror, romantic comics, missal.

The maid is sunning rectangles of white cloth on the bushes behind the house. I ask her what they are. She mutters something and moves off. They are bright with whiteness and soft to the touch. I suspect they are a private matter and ask no more about them.

VIII

The river—as I know it—runs from a dam at my cousins' sugar mill down to a pool at the bottom.

On Monday the women make their way to the river; balancing zinc washtubs on a braided cloth on their heads—this cloth has an African name. They take their places at specific rocks and rub, beat, wet, ring, and spread their laundry in the sun. And then leave. The rocks are streaked white after their chore is finished.

This is *our* land, *our* river—I have been told. So when women wash their clothes above the place where I swim; when the butcher's wife cleans tripe on Saturday morning; when a group of boys I do not know are using *my* pool—I hate them for taking up *my* space.

I hate them for taking up space; I hate them for not including me.

IX

The butcher's wife—after she has cleaned the tripe—comes to wax the parlor floor. She has a daughter my age who today is embarrassed and angry: I think it is because she is wearing one of my old dresses.

(Twenty years later I find she is part of us: "from" my great-uncle.)

There are many mysterious births here:

Three people come up to the steps and ask for my grandfather (who by this time is almost dead)—I am suspicious and question them closely. My grandmother explains: "They are your grandfather's *outside* children."

X

Three women—sisters, my second cousins; unmarried; middle-aged—live across the river. They have a plant called "Midnight Mystery" on their verandah. They come late one night to fetch me and we walk down the path, our way lit by a small boy with a bottle lamp. We balance ourselves across the river and reach the house—in time to see the large white flower unfold.

XI

One reason the parlor floor is waxed on Saturday is that my grandmother holds church on Sunday. People arrive at nine and sit for two hours: giving testimony, singing hymns, reading scripture. They sip South African wine and eat squares of white bread.

Religion looms: Zinc roofs rock on Sunday morning.

XII

The river "comes down": the dam breaks; rocks shift; animals are carried along.

The clouds build across the mountains and move into our valley. Then it rains. Over the rain I can hear the noise of the river. It *is* a roar; even the gully, which pays the river tribute, roars—and becomes dangerous.

This is clear power.

XIII

We cook on a woodstove in a kitchen behind the house. Our water is taken from the river in brimming kerosene tins. We read by lamp and moon light.

XIV

On one hillside next to the house is the coffee piece: the bushes are low, with dark-green leaves and dark-red fruit. Darkness informs the place. Darkness and damp. Tall trees preserve the dark. Things hide here.

I pick coffee for my grandmother. To be gentle is important: the bushes are sensitive. I carefully fill my basket with the fruit.

XV

After the birth of each of my grandmother's five children the cord was buried and orange trees planted near the house. These trees now bear the names of her children.

XVI

One child died—a son, at eighteen. His grave is in the flower garden, shaded by the orange trees. She tends the grave often, singing "What a Friend We Have in Jesus."

The walls of my grandmother's parlor are decorated with two photographs: of her two remaining sons.

XVII

My mother is my grandmother's daughter. My acquaintance with my mother in this house is from the schoolbooks stored in boxes underneath. Worms have tunneled the pages, the covers are crossed with mold—making the books appear ancient. She has left me to find her here, under this house: I seek identity in a childish hand and obsolete geography.

XVIII

A madwoman steals my grandfather's horse and tries to ride away. I know several madwomen here. She is the boldest; riding bareback, naked. The others walk up and down, talking to themselves and others. One talks to a lizard in the cashew tree at the bottom of the yard. Another sits in the river, refusing to cross.

This woman—one of my cousins—tells me twenty years later about her terror of leaving her place; about the shock treatments the family arranges in town; about how she kept the accounts; about her sister's slow death and how she cared for her.

It must have meant something that all those mad were women. The men were called idiots (an accident of birth); or drunks.

The women's madness was ascribed to several causes: childlessness, celibacy, "change": such was the nature of their naive science.

XIX

An old woman who sometimes works for us has built a house by the roadside. It is built of clay—from the roadbed—with wood for structure. It has a thatch roof and rests on cement blocks. It is one-room.

She promises to make me a cake if I help her paper the walls. I arrive early, my arms filled with newspapers. We mix flour paste and seek suitable stories for decoration. Pleased with our results, we gather flowers and put them in gourds around the room. True to her word, she bakes me a cake in an empty condensed milk tin.

XX

Walking down to the shop by the railway crossing, saying good morning, people stop me and ask for my mother—often mistaking me for her.

XXI

I want to visit my mother's school where she broke her ankle playing cricket and used the books which now lie under the house. I can't get to the school but I play cricket; using a carved bamboo root as she did and the dried stalk of a coconut tree for a bat. I play on the same pitch she used—a flat protected place across the road.

XXII

Walking through the water and over the rocks, I am exploring the river—eating bitter susumba and sweet valencia oranges. Up past pools named for people who drowned there; to the dam; to the sugar mill where I get wet sugar.

XXIII

What is here for me: where do these things lead:
warmth
light
wet sugar
rain and river water
earth
the wood fire
distance
slaughter
mysterious births
fertility
the women at the river
my grandmother's authority with land and scripture
a tree named with my mother's name.

Twenty years these things rush back at me: the memories of a child inside and outside.

XXIV

Behind the warmth and light are dark and damp/ behind the wet sugar, cane fields/behind the rain and river water, periods of drought/underneath the earth are the dead/underneath the wood fire are ashes to be

emptied/underneath the distance is separation/under-
neath the slaughter is hunger/behind the mysterious
births is my own/behind the fertility are the verdicts
of insanity/behind the women at the river are earlier
women/underlying my grandmother's authority with
land and scripture is obedience to a drunken husband/
under a tree named with my mother's name is a rotted
cord.

Accurate Record

Emma, being the eldest sister, had many things the baby could not have; but Emma, being a good girl, gave her little sister leave to look at all her toys, and you cannot think how pretty it was to see Emma lead her little sister by the hand and show her all her things. She used to say, "See here, dear little sister, look at this pretty thing; do not break it, my love; if you do, I shall not have another like it, and then I know you will be very sorry . . ."

Sometimes the little girl would want to keep Emma's toys too long, and Emma would want them: but she did not snatch them, saying instead, "I must teach her to be good and kind by being good and kind myself, and mama will love us more and more, every day . . ."

—The Little Sisters: or Emma and Caroline
(1840)

This is about my sister; about our childhood; about being the eldest of two daughters; about sentimentality; about separation; about the need for knowledge of origins; about obscure legends.

22

I

Hoisted on our father's shoulders—in a photograph shot by our mother under duress—I look at us now: then: six and two. That day in the park is a clear recollection: black gravel in our shoes; blue dragonflies on the surface of the lake; the car with the running board and the plaid divider in the backseat. (Behind us was the hospital for "defective" children.)

In this album there are no pictures of my broken wrist or my mouth cut open by the top of an orange juice can. There are no pictures of her split chin or her smashed front teeth. These pictures show only tense joy. This is not an accurate record at all.

II

The accurate record lies behind the smiles. It begins with the woman who took the picture: She and I are seated on a spread-out blanket in a field—before my sister's birth; pieces of clear and cobalt glass, chipped bits of flowered china laid on braided grass mats are arranged around us: we have made a feast for the dolls—at teatime.

Chestnut hair, dark eyes, accented speech, a face like mine—dark blood of which I was not told: denied knowledge of her body and her blood.

III

My mother is twenty-six when my sister is born: Black hair in a white bassinette. Eyes shut. They seat me on a sofa and place her in my arms.

(A dream: from my journal: August 2, 1977:
My mother and I are in a car. She is going to tell me
why she has kept things from me. Why she has kept her-
self from me. "I wouldn't have kept things from you if
they hadn't cut off my breast at twenty-six." She shows
me the space—which is smooth with only small white
scars—like the scars from arrow-wounds, I think.)

IV

We are in a walled garden where the plants need water;
where the sundial has rusted. The house attached to the
garden—where we live in close quarters—is a carriage
house, with alcoves and a slanting roof. Our bed fits into
an alcove next to a window. In this bed we enact our
fantasies:

a tent in a jungle clearing; as doctor and nurse we mend
survivors from a crashed plane.
a ship in dangerous waters tosses; sharks approach; we
beat them back.
a covered wagon crossing the Great Plains; our children
have fevers; food runs short; we must make it over the
Rockies before the snow.

V

We are two daughters divided, according to adjectives:
passive/active; dependent/independent; loving/aloof—

(We were not responsible for these divisions but we
lived them through.)

And yet they dress us alike; and we look nothing alike.
We are "river and sea" in the words of an uncle.

She is the final child—small and dark, nonmale—the daughter of the mother. I am the first—slim and tall; named for our father, whose daughter I become. We have the eyes of our respective parents.

VI

I have measles and so am isolated. I read Sherlock Holmes and listen to stories on the radio. She carries her chair to the doorway of the room, and sits relentless, watching—asking me if I feel better. My reaction is to snap: leave me alone.

(For years I never think beyond this apparent cruelty.)

VII

Our dead pets: our cats and dogs run over, lost in fights, the uninoculated victims of distemper.

A particular kitten is brought home by our father one Saturday afternoon—small, gray, striped, shaking. My sister, about six, wraps her in a towel and sits holding her for hours. I envy her unselfconscious singing to the kitten. But soon the cat dies and she is told that she has held her too tightly.

VIII

A birthday party: we are both invited; I am twelve, she is seven or eight. For some reason she begins to cry during the party—sitting alone at first; then, others gather around her and ask what's wrong. The mother of the birthday child approaches me and tells me to help my sister. I cannot. Instead I phone our father to come and get us.

Once home, I tell what has happened and use the word "ashamed"—the only word I can think of at the time: "I was ashamed of her." I feel the sharpness of his hand across my face and his words: "Don't you *ever* say that."

IX

The mail arrives. We are eleven and seven. A battle ensues over who shall sort the letters to our parents. She throws a patterned candy dish, hitting me in the head. I fall over, faking death to scare her. She bends over me; ruthless, I do not respond. I lie there and the house is quiet. She has left. I walk through the city after her, having no idea where she has gone; without thinking, I have taken my air rifle with me. I am powerless with this gun which fires only air; people notice me, this armed female eleven-year-old—their attention embarrasses me. I do not find her. Hours later she is found with a friend of our parents.

(Years later she will become a runaway and I will consider myself at fault.)

X

She is eight. I am twelve. Our parents are leaving us with two other people. The plane sits on the runway. Behind is the wreckage of another plane—an extraordinary setting for being left. As their plane lifts off we feel a similar impact. Suddenly she and I begin to cry. Together we weep for hours, not knowing when they will send for us; passing time meanwhile.

XI

I am twenty. She is sixteen. I tell the intern I am "in loco parentis"—that exact Latin phrase. Our parents are away and she has taken LSD. Sitting on their bed she screams as I approach her, telling me I am turning to stone—and tries to fly from the window at the end of the hall. Her arms and legs flail; she loses her shoes. They restrain her and run a red tube down her throat. Outside the room where she is, I sit, *Tender Is the Night* open in my lap: "do you mind if I pull down the curtain" read over and over again.

XII

My sister has a daughter when I am twenty-eight.

(from my journal: August 22, 1977:
A dream last night: I was in a bed-sitting room in London—the same place where I spent six months in 1971. It was a large dark room; it had a vast deep-red carpet on the floor. I was miscarrying on the carpet. What came forth—what I expressed—was a small fetus, female, covered in blood. I picked her up and began to lick the blood from her tiny very pale body. But there was a lot of blood and I couldn't quite get her clean. I began to kiss her on the mouth and realized she was not breathing. I started to convert the kisses to resuscitation—filling her lungs with my own breath. I remember that I thought, I have begun a relationship with this

27

child and now she's dead and I can't bring her back. I thought what does someone do in these circumstances. To dispose of her body in a plastic garbage bag or to slip her into the toilet down the hall is impossible. I must give her a proper burial.)

XIII

(Among the records of colonial India is the story of two "wild" sisters—found in a cave guarded by a she-wolf: whose body their "rescuers" pierced with arrows.)

Fearsome of the light; blind during day-hours—the sisters crouched and howled in the darkness, seeking meat at night-time.

These sisters moved on knees and elbows; or sped on feet and hands—away from invaders; or else confronted them with arched backs, heads shaking back and forth.

When the younger sister died, we are told the elder cried—for the first time—and did not take anything into herself for two days; and remained in her corner for a week; and for eleven days sniffed for the scent of the other.

After her period of mourning—the elder developed a vocabulary of fifty words; a liking for salt; a fear of the dark.

Against Granite

It is a marble building—but like a cave inside.

In the basement—against granite—a woman sits in plain sight. She is black: and old. "Are you a jazz singer?" someone asks. "No—a historian."

Archives are spread on the table where she works: complicated statistics of imprisonment; plans of official edifices; physiognomic studies of the type.

She is writing a history of incarceration.

Here is where black women congregate—against granite. This is their headquarters; where they write history. Around tables they exchange facts—details of the unwritten past. Like the women who came before them— the women they are restoring to their work/space—the historians are skilled at unraveling lies; are adept at detecting the reality beneath the erasure.

Out back is evidence of settlement: a tin roof crests a hill amid mountains—orange and tangerine trees form a natural border. A river where women bathe can be seen from the historians' enclave. The land has been cultivated; the crops are ready for harvest. In the foreground a young black woman sits on grass which flourishes. Here women pick freely from the trees.

(This is all in the primary line of vision. Not peripheral, but plain.)

Around the periphery are those who would
enforce silence:
slicers/suturers/invaders/abusers/sterilizers/infibulators/
castrators/dividers/enclosers—

traditional technicians/technicians of tradition.

Those who practice on women/those who practice
     on children:
The providers of Depo-provera:
     the deprivers of women's lives.
The promoters of infant formula:
     the dealers in child-death.
The purveyors of starvation and mutilation—there is no way else to say it.

Because peripheral, the border guards are shadowy— their features indistinct. They wear no uniforms, only name-tags: Upjohn, Nestle, Riker's, Welfare, Rockland State, Jesus, the Law of the Land—and yes, and also— Gandhi and Kenyatta.

The historians—like those who came before them— mean to survive. But know they may not. They know that though shadowy, the border guards have influence, and carry danger with them. And with this knowledge, the women manage.

And in the presence of this knowledge the historians plant, weed, hoe, raise houses, sew, and wash—and continue their investigations: into the one-shot contraceptive; the slow deaths of their children; the closing-up of vulvas and the cutting-out of tongues. By opening the sutures, applying laundry soap and brown sugar, they draw out the poisons and purify the wounds. And maintain vigilance to lessen the possibility of reinfection.

Each evening at dusk, the women gather under the tin roof which shelters the meeting-house: the progress notes of the day's work are read—then they cook dinner, talk, and sing: old songs whose noise carries a long distance.

A History of Costume

In the foreground a bird with a beautiful plume
circles round and round as if lost or giddy. There
are red holes in its head where there should be
eyes. Another bird, tied to a stake, writhes inces-
santly, for red ants devour it. Both are decoys . . . .
It is in the nesting season that the plumes are
brightest, so, if we wish to go on making pictures,
we must imagine innumerable mouths opening and
shutting, until—as no parent bird comes to feed
them—the young birds rot where they sit. Then
there are the wounded birds, trailing leg or wing,
as they flutter off to droop or falter in the dust.
But perhaps the most unpleasant sight that we
must make ourselves imagine is the sight of the
bird tightly held in one hand while another pierces
the eyeballs with a feather. But these hands—are
they the hands of men or of women?

—Virginia Woolf, "The Plumage Bill,"
The Woman's Leader, July 23, 1920

In the basement of the museum finery is on display; a
history of costume, open to the public. Plaster models—
their heads swathed in varicolored nylon stockings—are
placed in rooms dedicated to periods of time.

I

My mother and I meet in public places—and move be-
tween the swathed heads:
the faceless heads and covered bodies
the covered faces, the emblazoned bodies
the paisley-shawled bodies cut off from
the undistinguished heads.

We came to this exhibit in part to connect, in part to
recollect—but we hold few memories in common; and
our connections are limited by silences between us. Our
common ground is the island where we were born—and
we speak in the language spoken there. And we bear a
close resemblance, except for eye-color.

II

We move into a room
filled with fans
    corsets
    parasols
    shoes
the covering of birds/the perimeters of whales/handles
made from the tusks of elephants/the work of the silk-
worm: to receive the lotusfoot.

The tiny shoes are lush: carefully designed,
    painstakingly executed.
Green silk bordered in red,
    embroidered with golden birds in flight.
Sewn perhaps by a mother for her daughter,
    according to custom.
And according to custom, also,
    fitted by that mother over time.

III

I start to talk about these feet, but our conversation slides into another room, where a court dress of the eighteenth century is displayed: lapis blue silk sewn with silver; cinched waist; hips spread outward supported by a cage; breasts suggested by slight plaster mounds; small hands gesture toward the throat—no legs are visible.

Behind this dress is a painting: Adélaïde Labille-Guiard—*Portrait of the Artist with Two Pupils* (1785). The artist is at the center of the composition, before a canvas; two students stand behind her, women. The artist, later absorbed into silence, meant this work to show her dedication to teaching women; devised a state plan for female education. And her work, because of her intent, was considered radical and dangerous.

I want to talk about this woman's work, but the painting hangs here because of what she wears; and this is what my mother notices.

IV

These rooms are crowded—with artificial light, canned music—women wander past the work of women become the trappings of women. Which women turned the birds-of-paradise into a knee-length frock?—the life-work of creatures worn during one evening. By whose direction? Who trapped the birds? What decoys were employed? Who killed them?

V

In a corner of one room are enormous ornamental combs. From a wall an etching mocks as women topple—fooled into imbalance. But look again: It is the women-alone who fall—at the left, serenely upright, a woman walks supported by a man; at the right a deliveryman hurries, a gigantic package carried on his head.

Together my mother and I remember women with filled market baskets; women who carry a week's wet laundry from the washing place; a woman we know who bears water on her head—each day for half a mile. And briefly—recalling the women of our common ground—we meet.

VI

And then the wigs: the hair of another woman. Jo's chestnut hair cut off. The plumage of an ostrich. To wear another woman's hair. To wear the feathers of a large flightless bird. To cover a head with hair that has been sold.

The women of Marie Antoinette's court—their elevated heads; and the rats they say lived in them. We talk about teased hair: knotted, split, sprayed hair; bleached, dyed, kinked, straightened, curled hair. My mother's hair streaked blonde.

VII

Inevitably we change places with the displays: How did they sit? How did they walk? How did they get their waists so small?

We see ourselves in riding habits: black velvet coat with thick red roses—the jacket of Queen Alexandra; heavily

veiled top hat; high leather boots and slender crop—
seated askew, the body placed to one side. Would we
slide off? Would we use the whip? The first time—would
we wash the blood off, or let it fade?

VIII

In a dimly lit room are camisoles, slips, all other under-
things: these are soft cotton, pale flowers embroidered
and connected with gentle pastel ribbons. I imagine
women dressing and undressing—together in their white
eyelet cotton camisoles, helping each other undo the
ribbons. Perhaps napping during the afternoon of a
nineteenth-century house party—lying side by side on
large pillows, briefly released. Perhaps touching;
stroking the ribcage bruised by stays; applying a hanky
dipped in bay rum to the temples of another. Perhaps
kissing her forehead after the application is done—
perhaps taking her hand. Head on another's shoulder,
drifting. To be waked too soon. I like to think of
women making soft underclothes for their comfort;
as they comfort each other.

IX

This dream is interrupted by the crimson silk pajamas
of a harem woman: purple brocade coat trimmed in
gold braid and galloon; coins suspended above her eyes.

X

This meeting-place is filled with stolen gold, silver, coral,
pearls; with plundered skins, shells, bones, and teeth.
Aspects of ornamental bondage, all used to maintain
the costume.

XI

We reach the end of the exhibit: in a corner (American, nineteenth century) are a mourning couple; mother and daughter in identical black garb—the head of the mother swathed in black net; the tragedy of bombazine on a five-year-old likeness holding her mother's mourning hands.

Women's Work

I

The breastmilk of a scrubwoman mixes with the darkening water in a galvanized tin bucket—spreads with the suds across the floor—mingles with the residue of daytime residents—tracked in.

Between chairlegs she moves—pushes aside heavy oaken desks—crawling across black and white tiles she reaches the toilets. This is Chicago—the early part of this century.

At five a.m. the chill seeps into her wet dress as she waits to go home.

In Jamaica in the 1820s a slavewoman is found with roots and leaves she has gathered—arranged around her: slowly pounding the elements together in a hollowed-out calabash. She is preparing a solution.

In her cabin at night a blackwoman chooses abortion. But she is caught—her penalty: an iron collar to be worn until her child is born.

Glasgow 1856.
Back against a quieted loom, the spinner shifts—
then shuts her eyes against the hands of the supervisor—
submits—
her own hands grasp the frame—
plait a pattern in the dangling threads—
left over from another woman's shift:
an artwork of necessity.

On a postcard a row of blackwomen stand—
trackwomen of the B&O—
with shovels ready to dig a railroad bed.
It is wartime and manpower is short.
These women range in age—and dress—
yet all wear slacks.
They leave behind kitchens—not just their own.
Children—not just their own.
And rows and rows of other people's land.

They are here for the "duration."

An abbess in fifteenth-century Bologna decides on strict
rules for closure. Heavy curtains divide the nuns from
those who visit—and no one may lodge within.

The abbess dies. The nuns exhume her body—seat her in
a chapel they build themselves—and decorate the walls
with her paintings.

And worship her.

They report this all to the bishop—
saying her fingertips are still pink.

The abalone fisherwoman stands in her wet red cloth—
her knife held in her teeth—full basket—her friend
kneels alongside.

And in New York Sakiko Ide:
knife held against chrysanthemum—
slicing the bloom in two.

In Malaysia in an electronics factory a woman sees a
spirit in her microscope—another woman's face. Along
the line she alerts the other workers—there is excite-
ment: their mothers' likenesses have come to disrupt
production.

The owners call this a "subconscious wildcat strike."

France 1590.
A woman is laboring in fire.
The child emerges between her legs.
Flames lick and sear their flesh.
Looking down she sees what she has done:
"another witch the less."

India 1979. Satyrani Chadha finds her daughter; the
bulge of the child is not apparent: "There were no eyes,
no mouth . . . it was just a twisted black bundle lying in
a corner . . . the mother-in-law . . . told me to pick up
my rubbish and clear her courtyard."

I built these images of knowledge—
of remains.
of burying grounds.
>   Of Quemadero de la Cruz where scholars thought
>   they had discovered a new geological strata running
>   the length of a city and looked closer and found
>   teeth and hair and fat and bits of cloth mixed in—
>   welded together.

Ravensbrück combines with Troy.

of belladonna: clean cloths.
    Julia Stephen advising a tender preparation
      of the dead.
    Assata Shakur demanding to birth herself.
    Florence Nightingale draining wounds.
    Ethel Rosenberg cradling a prostitute
      at the Women's House of Detention.

of forces underground.
    Harriet Tubman with her gun.
    Susan B. Anthony with her gun.
    Burns removed by boiling white vinegar
      in the pan.
    Whispered instructions—
    the radical rose with its black center.

But also:
    The mother-in-law burning
    the daughter-in-law:
    while the son has a glass of milk.

II

The stakes in the square one afternoon in Augsburg
were so thick it seemed to be a forest: We are still learn-
ing to recognize what we see.

Traces erased. Details removed.
Letters sewn into quilts—or burned.
Self-portraits hidden in trunks—or burned.

The perishable nature of so many of our artifacts.

Shrines erected over shrines.
The line replaces the circle.

If we do these things to remember witches
If in our remembrance we find the depth of our history
Will we opt for description only
or choose to ignite the fuse of our knowledge?

III

"Whales Lure Scientists with Their Friendliness"—the
headline reads. Gray whales are traveling south. We see
them from the car—their sweet skins surface side by
side. Slick with wetness—streaked white from salt. They
carry barnacles—responsible for life outside, as well as
life within.

We are two women traveling south. And court these
female pairs.

There's a need for romance in this work.

We are two women traveling over backroads one eve-
ning. Past the farm which raises Arabian stallions. We
will be apart soon and need this evening. Your hand
rests lightly on my leg—"go slower," you ask. I pull off
the road to let the pick-up bearing down pass us.

On a dirt road now, I glance back. Two cars are parked
at its mouth. The road becomes a cow-path. I turn.
Headlights glare. The cars are in front and behind us.
"Hey, honey, want some?" a driver yells—

I reason: gang-rape. I reason: maybe guns.
I spin the car wheels. Somehow get out.
It is that quick.

There's a need for rage in this work.

Claiming an Identity
They Taught Me
to Despise

"Was anyone in this class not born in the United States?" the teacher asked us in the fifties. I was in third grade. I stood up and mumbled, "Jamaica," and became the focus of their scrutiny. I filled their silence with rapid lies.

Still in the third grade, I am kept after school for talking. My mother—young and thin, a pale gray coat which falls from squared-off shoulders, her brown hair long and turned under at her neck—comes to fetch me. As she confronts the teacher I begin to cry, my guilt and shame at bringing her into this strange place overcomes me.

I want to protect her from their scrutiny and what they will never understand.

I

> Bertha! Bertha! The wind caught my hair and it streamed outward like wings. It might bear me up, I thought, if I jumped to those hard stones.
>
> —Jean Rhys, *Wide Sargasso Sea*

Grace Poole gave him a cord, and he pinioned [her arms] behind her: with more rope, which was at hand, he bound her to a chair.

—Charlotte Brontë, *Jane Eyre*

pinion: the distal part of a bird's wing, including the carpus, the metacarpus, the phalanges; a wing—*as a noun*.

pinion: to cut off the pinion of a wing to prevent flight; to disable or restrain by binding the wings or arms, especially close to the body; to bind the wings or arms of; to shackle; to confine—*as a verb*.

To imagine I am the sister of Bertha Rochester. We are the remainders of slavery—residue:
    white cockroaches
    white niggers
    quadroons
    octoroons
    mulattos
    creoles
    white niggers.

Her hair became wings with the interference of the wind. And she smashed *on those hard stones.* Did the sockets pain her as *he bound her to a chair* with his swift and assured grasp? And Grace Poole, the alcoholic female keeper: what were her thoughts?

Pressed into service, moved into the great house—
    early on.
Daughters of the masters/whores of the masters
At one with the great house/
    at odds with the great house
Setting fire to the great house/ the masters/
    sometimes ourselves.

Early on I worried about children. Tales of throwback were common. Tell-tale hair, thick noses and heavy mouths—you could be given away so easily. Better remain unbred.

II

> *creole:* (the Fr. form of *criollo*, a West Indian, probably a negro corruption of the Span. *criadillo*, the dim. of *criado*, one bred or reared, from *criar*, to breed, a derivative of the Lat. *creare*, to create.) . . . It is now used of the descendants of non-aboriginal races born and settled in the West Indies, in various parts of the American mainland, and in Mauritius, Réunion, and some other places colonized by Spain, Portugal, France, or . . . by England . . . . The use of the word by some writers as necessarily implying a person of mixed blood is totally erroneous; in itself "creole" has no distinction of colour; a creole may be a person of European, negro, or mixed extraction— or even a horse . . . . The difference in type between the creoles and the European races from which they have sprung, a difference often considerable, is due principally to changed environment—especially to the tropical or semi-tropical climate of the lands they inhabit.
>
> —*Encyclopedia Britannica*, 11th edition

They can always fall back on the landscape—the sudden storms—the sun which burns even as it warms. The *changed environment* of red dirt, volcanic sand, sea-eggs whose spikes wash out with piss. Alligators. Jellyfish. Oysters who cling to pilings, to be sliced off with the sharp stroke of the *machete*. The high grass of sugar cane etching fine lines into bare legs. The extravagant blossoms which release strange aromas into the too-warm air. The bright moonlight spun with these perfumes. These are their clichés—a thin film covering the real.

To imagine I am the sister of Annie Palmer
"white witch"
creole bitch
imported to the north coast of Jamaica—
legend of the island
mistress of Rose Hall
guilty of husband-murder three times over.

We drove past Rose Hall often when I was a child. They repeated her life to me. They indicated the three coconut trees she used for grave-markers. They told me she practiced *obeah* and drank the white-men's blood for power and slept with the black overseer who killed her for infidelity.

And a rich Jamaican family bought the staircase where she died and instructed their servants not to wash the blood off.

My blood commenced early. The farther back you go the thicker it becomes. And the mother is named the link, the carrier—the source of the Nile. Did she attend each birth with caution? Waiting to see the degree of our betrayal?

"Pork!" the streetcleaner called.
Pigskin scraped clean.
"You not us. You not them either."

III

I find a broadside from nineteenth-century America.

The statement: *a creole may be . . . even a horse* is illuminated.

RAFFLE

> Mr. Joseph Jennings respectfully informs his friends and the public that, at the request of many acquaintances, he has been induced to purchase from Mr. Osborne of Missouri, the celebrated **Dark Bay Horse, "Star,"** aged five years, square trotter and warranted sound: with a new light Trotting Buggy and Harness. Also the dark, stout **Mulatto Girl, "Sarah,"** aged about twenty years, general house servant, valued at *nine hundred dollars,* and guaranteed, and **will be raffled for** at 4 o'clock p.m., February first, at the selection hotel of the subscribers. The above is as represented and those persons who may wish to engage in the usual practice of raffling, will, I assure them, be perfectly satisfied with their destiny in this affair.

They name us. They buy us and sell us.

I am twenty-two and sitting in my mother's kitchen. She is about to inform me "officially." I question her delay. "I didn't think it mattered"—as if to say, "I didn't think you'd mind." "You don't know what it was like when we first came here. No one wanted to be colored. Your father's family was always tracing me. And these Americans, they just don't understand. My cousin was fired from her job in a department store when they found out she was passing. I stopped seeing her because your father was always teasing me about my colored cousin. Things are different now. You're lucky you look the way you do, you could get any man. Anyone says anything to you, tell them your father's white."

IV

> I wish to stay here in the dark . . . where I belong.
>
> *—Wide Sargasso Sea*

I dreamed there was a record album called *Black Women*. The front of the album was a baroque painting depicting a galleon on rough seas—sailing over a dragon which was visible on either side of the bow. Inset was the portrait of a large light-skinned woman—in a white turban and plain white bodice: dressed as a slave. This woman was also at the helm of the galleon and was identified in fine writing as the first black navigator. The painting, the writing continued, had been taken from a manuscript entitled *Emergam,* Munich, 1663. The dream continued—I interviewed two white women historians who told me the manuscript had been proved a fake. We argued about the false and the real but they were adamant.

(Emergam is the first-person future of the Latin verb *emergere:* to rise up, emerge, free oneself.)

V

> These pictures were in watercolours. The first represented clouds low and livid, rolling over a swollen sea: all the distance was in eclipse; so too was the foreground; or, rather, the nearest billows, for there was no land. One gleam of light lifted into relief a half-submerged mast, on which sat a cormorant, dark and large, with wings flecked with foam; its beak held a gold bracelet, set with gems . . . a drowned corpse glanced through the green water; a fair arm was the only limb clearly visible, whence the bracelet had been washed or torn.
>
> *—Jane Eyre*

This is the vision of Jane Eyre, small and pale. She is speaking of us. We dwell in the penumbra of the eclipse. In the half-darkness. They tell us the dark and light lie beyond us. "I feel sorry for you," the dark woman said, "You don't know who you are."

The ship in the vision has foundered. The cormorant has taken her place and surveys the damage. Her dark plumage is wet, so we know who has taken the bracelet from the white woman's arm. *The large dark bird sits with wings pinioned in the wooden chair.*

It would seem the cormorant has replaced the dragon in my dream: but no, she is the navigator, expressed by another, stripped of her power. She nests on high and dives deep into warm waters. She has green eyes and is long-lived. (It came down to this: my eyes might save me. Green-blue. Almost blue. Changing with each costume.)

VI

I have seen the wreckage of sugar mills covered with damp and green mosses. When the concrete cracks across, green veins trace the damage. There are tracks where mules used to circle—to crush the cane. There are copper cauldrons once used to boil the juice, from which molasses and foam were drawn off to make rum. (The purest rum—do I have to say it?—is colorless and called white. Other rum is colored artificially, taking on the darkness of the casks over time—they think the golden tint makes it more appealing. The final type is colored by impurities and was once called Negro rum.)

There are great houses throughout this island abandoned to the forest.

A great aunt keeps a chipped crystal doorknob—a solid polyhedron—on the dining table of her pensioner's flat in England: "From our place at Dry Harbour," she explains. "Fancy . . . every door had one."

Wetness spreads through the wooden house. Damp spots emerge through French wallpaper where children spin thin hoops along gravel walkways. And women glide with frilled umbrellas. This is not part of us: this nineteenth-century scene of well-being. Better to look in the shacks built in the back, where newsprint covered the walls. And calendars advertised the English royal family.

VII

The white-haired woman sits with rice piled on her dinner plate. I am ten years old and we are visiting a branch of the family. She is my first encounter with the island I left when I was three. She is the first encounter I remember. "More rice!" she screams at the woman who serves the table. And rice is brought. "More rice!" again. My sister—who is six— and I giggle. There is a woman at the head of the table who screams for rice. The mound is high. The grains slide down the mound and onto the white cloth. "No more rice," she closes.

VIII

You are trying to make me into someone else, calling me by another name. I know, that's *obeah* too.

—*Wide Sargasso Sea*

50

The Alms House at May Pen is yellowing wood. It stands above a long flight of wooden steps with a narrow handrail. There is—whenever we pass—a crowd at the top of the stairs, gathered in the yard of the Alms House. I always ask about these people. Somewhere I have confused them with lepers. "Are they lepers?" I ask my father. "No, not lepers; just people with no place to go."

The Garden

I

Not a walled place—in fact, open on all sides.
Not secret—but private.
A private open space.

I trim the stakes to mark the rows—string a fence with
cord to support the snow peas—move rocks aside and
bits of porcelain, some plastic; each day there is more
to be taken away. Carefully dig to the required depth
for broccoli, lettuces—turn the eyes of limas and string
beans downward—mix the thin seeds of carrots with
sturdy radishes: "companionate planting"—one protects
the other. Basil alongside tomato. Garlic everywhere.

The man across the way, busy with his machine, ciga-
rette ash mixing with turned earth—is watching me.
I am wearing khaki shorts and a t-shirt which reads
Xantippe. He approaches, smiling, rolling across the
border. "Do you want me to go through with my
rototiller?" he asks. I concentrate on the old hoe I
found in the barn, and respond only after I have made
contact with the furrow. "No, thank you, I prefer to
work by hand." A smirk, then—"Anytime you change
your mind . . ." drifting off.

At first I didn't notice. But then a large footprint made me look further. His mark across the rows I had made yesterday. One enormous foot planted on a squash hill. And the traces of his mechanical sidekick zigzagging over lettuce, broccoli, chard. "I could kill," my only thought.

II

"I sometimes attack the ground, rather than moving in a smooth rhythm. When I garden, which is almost daily, I think at least once of my mother's challenge that everything will probably die, and so it's my challenge to assure that everything lives—my difficulty in thinning, *sentimental obstacle*. This goes to a deep place; to being told I was unloving and unnurturing as a child (and adult). I feel the weeds in the garden encroaching as a personal threat to my ability to nurture. I also feel them as my mother and sister encroaching on my life; so the plants become a metaphor for my own life and the powerful weeds (which seem to be able to endure anything) my mother's and sister's demands. So my gardening is a pitched battle against this; and is thus contaminated. I have also felt as I walk to the garden (in the middle of a meadow) that I am threatened; that there is a snake or animal lurking somewhere— that someday I will see this creature, and the garden will be spoiled.

"Last night, reading about Florence Nightingale—her final method to save herself from the unending encroachments of her mother and sister was to be ill. She had tried for many years to rid herself of their constant and insistent presence in and demands on her life. She never confronted the need for separation and worked through it—what she did was to remove

herself from them by (1) working herself almost to
the point of death; ridding them, by filling her life
and mind with other matters, which could not have
possibly interested them (yet she admittedly longed for
her mother's approval); and (2) when this was not
successful, by becoming ill every time they threatened
to come near, thus punishing herself also. . . . And so
I woke this morning with a pinched nerve in my neck
and my right arm numb. Partly physical, of course,
but I am experiencing it as a knot of unexpressed
anger which I have turned against myself—another
implosive reaction, like depression. The concept of
Nightingale by her mother and sister was so similar
to my own experience: autocratic, aloof, puritanical,
unloving, willing to devote her life to 'strangers' rather
than to 'family,' deviant, etc.

"How they 'accidentally' shut her pet owl, Athena,
in the attic and killed her—and how they taunted
Nightingale for loving her owl more than she loved
them."

(This was written about another garden.)

III

The rakish stripes of the potato bugs—hard back crush-
ing under a stone. Dull gray shell of the squash borer—
smashing one with two fingers, and thick blue milk
oozes forth. Bright orange eggs fast to the underside of
eggplant leaves—scraped off with a fingernail. Japanese
beetles plop into a coffee tin filled with turpentine.
Green cabbage worms succumb to a dusting of wood
ash. And tiny white flies scatter as a mist of water and
red pepper reaches them.

The books I use call these "natural controls." Still I fear that this hand-to-hand combat will be punished.

IV

The fleshy placenta of the bean-seed breaks the surface.

An article in the newspaper: a child with spina bifida—open spine. Thoughts of Susannah and her open-heart surgery. A child with Downs syndrome and a defective valve. Time spent with her and a desire to give myself over to her enormous needs totally—playing the *Red Back Book* for hours while she rocked in a corner and twirled her piece of silk. Each time the record finished—a scream. Also knowing the reality of her existence and how it is for her mother to have a child like her plus two other children. But she is the only kind of child I can imagine for myself. How she learned my name and slept with me—nose running on the quilt. I have no children and know I never will.

V

Ice crystals still in the grass.
The translucent skin of green tomatoes.
Squashes suspended.
It seems as if the plants drip—
an early frost.

Cutting back the leaves and stems of the basil plants—string beans—pea vines. Laying them on the compost heap—now that decomposition has begun. This is a strange destruction.

Women gone mad from childlessness—the philosophers talk about unfulfilled purpose—stray uterus rampaging—burning, cutting, slicing—discarding. *Immanence* and *inner space.* Our universe—the black hole—the void within.

Is the alternative Mary Wollstonecraft
with puppies at her breasts?
Charlotte Brontë vomiting to death?
Mariah Upshur holding Rabbit as the worms choke him?
The Virgin Mary with the dead Christ?

VI

I dream about my mother and sister. Both about to give birth. In a dark hospital staircase my mother hands me an enameled bowl—containing a piece of tissue and some blood. Not an abortion, not even a miscarriage—a child who will develop according to my care. My sister sits back, full belly stroked, while the tissue is delivered to me—in my care. I intentionally neglect it—letting it drown in its own piss.

VII

A history of women and gardens:
Dorothea Lange's ex-slave with a long memory. Dickinson kneeling on her folded red blanket, tending exotica. Fannie Lou Hamer standing in a cotton field. The Chrisman sisters before their sod house. Sibylla Merian escaping to Surinam to draw from life.

And Millet's *gleaners* and Raphael's *belle jardinière* and Wordsworth's *solitary reaper.*

The Garden

Market women in Jamaica, baskets hung across a don-
key's back while they walk alongside—a stick in hand
to urge the animal on—to Linstead, to May Pen, to Port
Maria. Hair spun into braids under a straw hat, tight
black eyes of ackees stare from raffia pods—fresh
dress—sneakers newly whitened. To sit or squat for
hours while they teach about their work.

My own grandmother: "I was very glad hearing from
you again, because your last letter said you intended
to live in the country, it's nice that you feel more
safe there, and you can plant your things and watch
them growing. That's what I always do when I was
younger, I loved to plant and see them growing, now
I am old I can't do these things anymore and besides
there is no land room, your uncle has the whole place
in citrus."

VIII

In this cold the spinach may bolt.
The broccoli continue.
The turnips fulfill their globes underground.

IX

To garden is a solitary act.

Separations

I dreamed I had two daughters—four and two years old.
The three of us are at the seaside (I say "seaside"
because the dream is set in the nineteenth century)
and I see that my daughters have no hands: just hollow
stumps at the ends of their arms. I leave them to play
in the sand and stroll along the boardwalk. I hide out
of their sight behind a brick wall and watch as tiny
hands descend from the hollow stumps. They giggle
together in their deceit of me.

I

My mother's effects lie divided around the house.
Heavy leaded crystal with discreet slashes in the bowl
and stem.
Six sizes.
White china—an incomplete set—trimmed in cobalt
blue and gold.
Dark-red enamel clock with a bell-jar shade.
Pieces of assorted Wedgwood.
A Rosenthal vase.
More crystal. Decanters. Pitchers. Bowls.
A tea set with square plates.

We are breaking up my mother's house. She sits—in the early American replica with the scarred arm— in her nightgown, although it's only seven on a Friday evening, telling us who should get what—while rolling her hair on pink curlers. She is far removed from us; now weeping, now recounting what has been done to her.

My mother has decided to live without her possessions. And I have been called to the distribution of the goods. My sister and my sister's daughter are here too.

We divide the goods, tape the cartons, wrap the things in newsprint, and seal the boxes.

II

"What shall we do with his chess sets?" "Let's sell them." "No." "Why not?" "The son of a bitch doesn't deserve to see them again." "No, we can't." "Why not?" "After what he's done to you . . ." "You've got to get angry and stop moaning." "You don't understand."

Chess. When I was six he taught me how to play. I'm not brave enough to use the Queen and keep her surrounded by pawns at my end of the board. Hoping he'll leave her alone. But he doesn't and I begin to cry. "You might as well quit now. Once you lose your Queen, checkmate is only a matter of time."

My sister and I are half-afraid he'll come through the door. We imagine guns. We imagine he'll be drunk. We imagine that if he wanted to kill himself he would take us with him. Yet he rarely struck us. And never hit our mother. Still we feel endangered. Neither of us can sleep that night. We stay up, rehashing his insanity.

"I don't know, Mom, I think we should sell them. You don't owe him anything." "No, we can't."

The chess sets remain in their glass case.

III

My mother brings forth two large cartons, puts them in front of us on the floor. Resumes her seat. "Letters and papers," she says. Opening one carton, pouring the contents out.

Unpaid bills—some way beyond the statute of limitations; report cards; photographs; his paycheck stubs; our diplomas; matchbooks; my awards and degrees; brochures of hotels; and every note, letter, or card he ever sent her: "With all my love," "To the greatest wife," "Happy birthday, sweetheart," "Hi, sexy"; and there are my letters from abroad.

"Tear everything up. Unless you want to keep something."

I wish she would leave us to do it. But of course she can't. As we begin the demolition, she watches. "Let me see that. Imagine that woman doing that to your father. How could he fall for that whore?"

IV

As I search for information about my father I find that hard gray stones have collected in my mind, whose surfaces reveal nothing. At times lights flash across these stones, but do not stay. Only now and then does one light focus on one stone which—with severe effort—

may crack. Then the light will play across the brilliant crystalline formations at the center of the memory, revealing essentials, creating shadows.

I once dreamed about these stones. I sat on a plateau in a mountain range and they hung from the sky all around me. One by one they dropped and smashed; and I felt imperiled by their centers.

My father taught me about exploration. About chivalry and conquest. Richard the Lionhearted. Napoleon. Cortez. He taught me to spell Tyrannosaurus Rex and Caesar Augustus and Timbuktu. And sang to me: "Danny Boy" at full volume. And recited poetry: "The Lady of Shalott." He spoke in Latin and told me about being brought up by the Jesuits, because he had no real family.

But there were other confidences. Many I cannot remember. And there were incidents—sitting in bars with a Coke while he went "somewhere." "Don't tell your mother we stopped here." And I never did.

V

I read in an ancient source about an unnamed woman— wife of a Roman citizen. Her mother was arrested and imprisoned. In fact, condemned to death—starvation in a small cell. A merciful sentence, because of her nobility. Her daughter was allowed to visit her, which she did daily, after being searched for food. She managed to sustain her mother's life by giving her full breasts to the prisoner.

The ancient source remarks that this is an unusual way for a daughter to feed her mother, and states further that the city of Rome was so impressed by the devotion of the younger woman that they let the older woman go free.

I cannot do this for my mother; not merely because I have no milk. I cannot do this for my mother. We have no proximity. My mother has no knowledge of my breasts. I approach her like the stereotype of a sleep-walker—arms outstretched to test the surroundings and avoid collision. I sleepwalked as a child: ran through the house, in and out of rooms. My mother screamed. She thought I was a ghost.

My mother did not nurse me, but my decision not to suckle her is not vengeful. She asks too much of me. She has no knowledge of my breasts, my clitoris, my intelligence.

VI

Among the relics spread on the floor is a formal photograph. A young girl poses in an embroidered silk dress; a watch hangs from a gold bow at her right shoulder. She wears a ring and a fine chain bracelet. Her hair is pinned in curls. Her face is unmade: calm. She has folded her arms over a rustic fence—a prop supplied by the photographer.

The photograph is mounted on cardboard, a fancy border framing the oval portrait.

I have had a history with this woman—she is not my mother: she exists in photographs. Occasional flashes of memory. The complicated indications of dreams.

My small hand traces the worn wicker of the train seat. (It is 1949.) She and I are traveling north together. In the memory I can almost see her face.

Dim afternoon light enters a room through closed shades. I am standing next to the bed where she rests. But I should be the one napping. Her flat chest breathes. I stand and watch her breath.

She is tall—her hair, wet from a swim in salt water, is pushed behind her ears. Her face is long: solemn. She has threaded a striped necktie through the waistband of her white trousers—like a cricketer announcing his affiliation. This is not a dream but a snapshot. Taken in the thirties.

Another photograph was taken after they removed both breasts. Re-covered the space they left with flesh from her thighs. Still, she died. In this picture she wears a Sunday dress, hat, gloves. Her face is thinner. Indistinct.

They tell me I stood in corners burning-in my mourning. Restrained myself against their embraces. I was three years old.

Now—I ask my mother about this woman who took care of me. No answer. She starts to cry. "Someday I'll be able to tell you. Not now."

VII

I have known other women with cancer—other women who died. Their deaths embedded in the tissues of their breasts or between their thighs. She becomes the model for them all.

Michelle Cliff

There is a final image: I am an infant, seated on the lap of a shrouded figure. A woman covered by a bedspread to look like a chair. The caption, written by my father, reads: "Baby and the ghost."

I have traveled with this ghost. I dream she is driving me through the places of my past. On a road a small child waits for us—dirty, pale, with open sores. The child approaches me, smiles: "Will you take me with you, this time?"

VIII

It is getting late. My sister and I continue—filling plastic bags, the contents carefully torn, so no one will know "our business." My mother and sister have decided to live together. And alone. Without my sister's daughter.

"We can't take care of her and ourselves." "And, besides, her father wants her." "She'll be better off with him." "We just can't manage, two women and a child." "I don't know how our happy little family could have come to this."

"Your aunt loved you so much. She didn't want to leave you. She wouldn't have died except she loved you and delayed the surgery too long. When they cut her open it was just too late."

I leave them to themselves.

64

Persephone Press, Inc. is a lesbian-feminist publishing house producing innovative and provocative writings to foster lesbian sensibility and new ways of thinking.

Choices
  Nancy Toder $6.00

The Coming Out Stories
  Julia Penelope Stanley,
  Susan J. Wolfe, editors
  Adrienne Rich, Foreword $6.95

A Feminist Tarot
  Sally Gearhart and Susan Rennie $5.00

The Wanderground: Stories of the Hill Women
  Sally Miller Gearhart $5.00

Woman, Church & State
  Matilda Joslyn Gage
  Sally Roesch Wagner, Introduction
  Mary Daly, Foreword $7.95